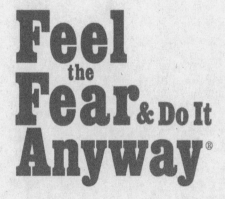

Feel the Fear & Do It Anyway®

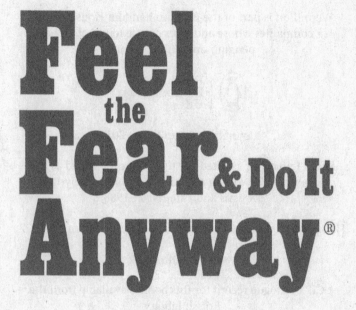

Feel the Fear & Do It Anyway®

Susan Jeffers, PhD

Vermilion
LONDON

5 7 9 10 8 6 4

Vermilion, an imprint of Ebury Publishing,
20 Vauxhall Bridge Road,
London SW1V 2SA

Vermilion is part of the Penguin Random House group
of companies whose addresses can be found at global.
penguinrandomhouse.com

Penguin
Random House
UK

First published in the United Kingdom by Vermilion in 1997

www.penguin.co.uk

A CIP catalogue record for this book is available from the
British Library

ISBN 9781785041129

Printed and bound in Great Britain by Clays Ltd, St Ives PLC

Penguin Random House is committed to a sustainable future
for our business, our readers and our planet. This book is
made from Forest Stewardship Council® certified paper.

Contents

Contents

Introduction

Fear seems to be everywhere in our lives. We fear beginnings, and we fear endings. We fear change, and we fear staying stuck. We fear success, and we fear failure. We fear living, and we fear dying.

This book will help you to find a way to deal with any fear. There are many ideas, exercises and tips in the book to help you learn how to ease away your fears. You will move to a place of power, energy and excitement.

Chapter 1

What Are You Afraid of ... and Why?

I know that some fear is natural and healthy and keeps us alert to trouble. The rest holds us back. It stops us growing, and is out of place and damaging. It can perhaps be blamed on how we were brought up. Fear can be broken down into three levels. The first level of fears is easy to see. Those fears are on the surface.

Look at the lists below where the first level of fears is divided into two types. There are those that just happen. And there are those that need action.

Level 1 Fears

Fears That Happen	Fears That Need Action
Getting old	Going back to school
Becoming disabled	Making choices
Retiring	Changing a career

Being alone

Children leaving home

Being caught up in a natural disaster, like a flood

Losing money and security

Something that matters changing

You or someone close to you dying

War breaking out

Suffering an illness

Losing a loved one

Having an accident

You or someone close to you being raped

Making friends

Ending or beginning a relationship

Having a child

Asserting yourself

Losing weight

Being interviewed

Driving

Public speaking

Making a mistake

Getting close to someone

The list does not include every fear. Different people have different fears. You might have a few fears you can add to the list. Many people fear some of the fears on the list. Some fear all of them. One aspect of fear is that it tends to spread through many areas of our lives. For example, if you fear making new friends, it is likely that you may also fear going to parties, having close relationships, applying for jobs, and so on.

This is made clearer by a look at the second level of fears. These fears are very different from those on Level 1. Level 2 fears are not based on what is going on around you. These fears involve the ego which means your sense of yourself. Here is a list of Level 2 fears

Level 2 Fears

Being rejected	Being tricked
Succeeding	Being helpless
Failing	Being disapproved of
Being at risk	Losing your image, or idea, of yourself

Level 2 fears have to do with *inner states of mind* rather than things happening to you. They reflect your sense of self and how you deal with the world. A Level 2 fear often leads to many other fears. If you are afraid of being rejected, this fear will affect almost every area of your life – friends, close relationships, job interviews, and so on.

Rejection is rejection – wherever it is found. If you can't deal with it, you begin to protect yourself, and as a result, greatly limit yourself. You begin to shut down and close out the world around you.

Look at the Level 2 list again, and you will see how any one of those fears can have a harmful affect on many areas of your life.

There is just one Level 3 Fear. It is the biggest fear of all – the one that really keeps you stuck. Are you ready?

Level 3 Fear

I can't handle it!

'That's it? That's the big deal?' you may ask. I know you are disappointed and wanted something much more dramatic than that. But the truth is this:

At the bottom of every one of your fears is simply the fear that you can't handle whatever life may bring you.

Let's test this. The Level 1 fears translate to:

- I can't handle illness.
- I can't handle making a mistake.
- I can't handle losing my job.
- I can't handle getting old.
- I can't handle being alone.
- I can't handle making a fool out of myself.
- I can't handle not getting the job.
- I can't handle losing him or her.
- I can't handle losing my money… etc.

The Level 2 fears translate to:

- I can't handle the worry of success.
- I can't handle failure.
- I can't handle being rejected… etc.

Level 3 is – simply, 'I can't handle it!'
  The truth is:

**If you knew you could handle anything
that came your way, what would you
possibly have to fear?**

The answer is: Nothing!

I know you are probably not jumping up and down for joy just yet, but believe me when I tell you I have just given you a great piece of news. What I have just told you means you can handle all your fears without having to control anything in the outside world. This should be a huge relief.

- You no longer have to control what your partner does.
- You no longer have to control what your friends do.
- You no longer have to control what your children do.
- You no longer have to control what your boss does.

- You no longer have to control what happens at an interview.
- You no longer have to control what happens at your job.
- You no longer have to control what happens in your new career.
- You no longer have to control what happens to your money.
- You no longer have to control what happens in the world.

All you have to do to lessen your fear is to gain more trust in your ability to handle whatever comes your way!

I am repeating the point because it is so critical. From this moment on, every time you feel afraid, remind yourself that it is simply because you are not feeling good enough about yourself. Then use one or more of the tools in this book to help build yourself up. You have your task clearly mapped out for you. There is no need to feel confused.

I have often been asked to explain why we have so little trust in ourselves. I do not really know the answer to that. But, it tends to begin when we are children.

I know that some fear is natural and healthy and keeps us alert to trouble. The rest holds us back. It stops us growing, and is out of place and damaging. It can perhaps be blamed on how we were brought up.

In all my life, I have never heard a mother say to her child 'Take a lot of risks today, darling,' as he or she goes off to school. She is more likely to say, 'Be careful, darling.' This 'Be careful' carries two messages: 'The world is really dangerous out there' *and* 'You won't be able to handle it.'

What Mum is really saying, of course, is, 'If something happens to you, *I* won't be able to handle it.' You see, she is only passing on her lack of trust in *her* ability to handle what comes her way.

I can remember wanting a two-wheeled bicycle and my mother refusing to buy me one. Her answer was always the same: 'I love you too much. I don't want anything to happen to you.'

I took this to mean: 'You are not clever enough to handle a two-wheeled bike.' Having become older and wiser, I realise now that she was really saying: 'If anything happens to you, I will fall apart.'

My very caring mother was once in hospital after serious surgery, with tubes down her nose and her throat. When I was told it was time for me to leave, I whispered in her ear that I loved her and would be back later. I didn't know if she could hear me or not. As I was walking towards the door, I heard a small, weak voice behind me saying – you guessed it – 'Be careful.'

Though she was dazed with drugs, she was sending me warnings of doom and gloom. And I know she is just like many mothers out there. When you think how many times our parents said, 'be careful', it is amazing we even managed to walk out the front door!

Our fear may or may not come from our parents. It may come from somewhere else. But does it really matter where our self-doubts come from? I believe not. I don't try to understand the causes of self-doubt and fear.

Even if I could work out the causes, that might not remove the fear. I believe that if something is troubling you, simply start from where you are and take the action needed to change it.

In this case, you know that lack of trust in yourself is stopping you from getting what you want out of life. And you know that you don't like that. Knowing this creates a very clear, even sharp, focus on what needs to be changed.

You do not have to waste your energy wondering why. It does not matter. What matters is that you begin now to build your trust in yourself, until you reach the point where you will be able to say:

**Whatever happens to me,
however awful, I can handle it!**

I can hear people out there doubting this. They are saying, 'Oh, come on now! How do you handle being disabled, or the death of a child, or cancer?' I understand your doubts. Remember that I was once doubtful myself.

Just read on and see what is in this book. Give yourself a winning chance by using the tools provided all through this book. As you do that, you will find yourself coming closer and closer to such a high level of confidence that you will begin to realise that you can handle *anything* that comes your way.

Never let these three little words out of your mind. They are possibly the most important three little words you'll ever hear:

I'll handle it!

Chapter 2

Can't You Make It Go Away?

Janet is still waiting for the fear to go away. She had always planned to return to college once her children were in school, but she now notices it has been four years since her youngest child entered Year Two. New excuses have popped up since that time: 'I want to be here when the children come home from school', 'We really don't have the money','My husband will feel that I don't care for him.'

Although it is true that certain plans would have to be worked out, that is not why she is nervous. In fact, her husband is willing to help her in any way he can. He is concerned about her sadness, and often urges her to fulfil her lifelong dream of becoming a fashion designer.

Each time Janet thinks about calling the local college to ask for an interview, something stops her. 'When I'm not so frightened, then I'll make the call.' 'When I feel a little better about myself, then I'll make the call.' It seems likely that Janet is going to wait a very long time.

The problem is that her thinking is all mixed up. The logic she uses will always cause her to fail. She will never break the fear barrier until she is made aware of her faulty thinking. She simply does not see what is obvious to those who are out there doing it.

Nor did I until I was forced to. Before my divorce, I was rather like a child, allowing my husband to take over the running of my life. After my divorce, I had to start doing things on my own. Small things, such as fixing the vacuum cleaner all by myself, gave me great pleasure. The first night I invited people to my home for dinner was a huge leap. When I booked tickets for my first trip without a man I was thrilled and felt proud.

As I began to *do* things on my own, I began to sense the delight of a new confidence. It was not all comfortable – in fact, a lot of it was very painful. I felt like a child learning to walk and often falling. But with each step I felt a little surer of my ability to handle my life.

As my confidence grew, I kept waiting for the fear to go away. Yet each time I tried something new, I felt frightened and unsure of

14

myself. 'Well,' I told myself, 'just keep trying. *Eventually* the fear will go away.' It never did! But one day I suddenly realised this truth:

TRUTH 1

The fear will never go away as long as I go on growing.

As long as I went on pushing out into the world, as long as I went on stretching my abilities, as long as I went on taking new risks to make my dreams come true, I was going to feel fear.

What a revelation! Like Janet, and so many of you reading this book, I had grown up waiting for the fear to go away before I took any chances. 'When I am no longer afraid... then I will ...!' For most of my life, I had played the WHEN/THEN game. And it never worked.

Once again, you are probably not jumping up and down with joy. I know that this idea is not exactly what you wanted to hear. You may have been hoping that my words of wisdom would work a miracle and make your fears go away. I am sorry to say it does not work that way. But, rather than thinking of this as a let-down, think of it as a relief. You no longer have to work so hard on getting rid of the fear. Because it is not going to go away!

But don't worry. As you build confidence in yourself with the exercises suggested in this book, your relationship with fear will change totally.

Not long after finding Truth 1, I found another important truth that helped me grow even further:

TRUTH 2

The only way to get rid of the fear of doing something is to go out and do it.

This might seem to conflict with Truth 1, yet it doesn't. Fear of *particular* things or events went away when I finally faced them. The 'doing it' comes *before* the fear goes away.

I can explain this by telling you about the first class I taught at a university. I was not much older than my students and I was teaching a subject which I didn't know at all well. I was teaching about what happens to people's minds when they get old.

I thought about the first class with a huge sense of dread. During the three days before the class, my stomach churned. It felt like it was on a roller coaster. I had prepared eight hours of work for a one-hour class. I had written enough pages for three classes. But this didn't take away my fear. When the first day of class finally arrived, I felt like I was going to die. As I stood in front of my students, I could feel my heart pounding and my knees shaking. Somehow I got through that class. But I wasn't really looking forward to the second one the following week.

Thankfully, things were easier the next time. (If they hadn't been, I might have left teaching for ever!) I started to know some of the faces in the classroom and to link some of the names to the faces. The third class was better than the second, as I started to relax and go with the flow of the students.

By our sixth class I was actually looking forward to standing in front of my students. Contact with my students was exciting and made me think in a fun way. One day, as I was walking towards that once dreaded classroom, I realised I was no longer afraid. Instead of feeling fear, I was looking forward to seeing my students and teaching them.

I had to teach many courses before I could walk into a class without detailed notes. But, after a while, all I had in my hand was a one-page outline of what I wanted to cover in that class. I realised how far I had come. I had felt the fear ... and done it anyway. So I got rid of my fear of teaching in classrooms. Yet, when I began teaching on television, again I felt fear. But, after I had done it often enough, I lost my fear of appearing on television. So it goes.

Another part of the WHEN/THEN game I used to play had to do with my self-esteem, which is another way of saying 'my ego' which means my sense of myself. I used to think: 'When I feel better about myself ... then I'll do it.' This is another mix-up in the order of how things happen. I kept thinking that if I could improve my self-esteem, then the fear would go away and I could start doing things.

I didn't know exactly *how* my self-esteem was going to improve. Perhaps by my growing older and wiser, or through feedback from other people, or a miracle would make me feel wonderful about myself. I even bought myself a belt buckle that read 'I'M TERRIFIC', thinking that through some strange process I'd get the message.

Maybe all those things did help a little. What really changed things, however; was the sense of pride I felt when I pushed through fear and did things on my own. Finally, this became clear:

TRUTH 3

The only way to feel better about myself is to go out... and do it.

The 'doing it' comes *before* the feeling better about yourself. When you make something happen, the fear of the thing or the event goes away, and you get a big bonus – you do a lot toward building your self-confidence. It's likely, however, that when you've finally done something properly and got rid of the fear, you will feel so good that you will decide there is something else out there you want to do. And guess what! The fear begins again as you prepare to try something else that is new.

I went to many workshops and lectures as I learned to deal with fear, and I found out something else that made me feel a whole lot better about myself:

TRUTH 4

It's not just me who feels fear when I do something new. Everyone else feels it too.

I said to myself: 'You've been jealous of all those people out there because they're not afraid to move ahead with their lives. And now you're saying that really they have been afraid all along? Why didn't somebody tell me!?' I guess I never asked. I was sure I was the only person out there feeling so hopeless. It was such a relief to realise I was not alone in this. I had the rest of the world to keep me company.

In 2016 Louise, the singer who found fame with the girl band Eternal, was on *Strictly Come Dancing*. Louise also had a long solo career as a singer. She is now a TV presenter and she is married to former footballer Jamie Redknapp. When she heard she would be on *Strictly Come Dancing*, Louise said this:

'I've sung in front of crowds of thousands before, but the idea of stepping out onto that famous dance floor with a world-class professional dancer gives me butterflies just thinking about it!'

If you are aware of the Fear Truths, Louise's fear will not surprise you. Ballroom dancing was an art that tested her in a new way, and of course she would be frightened. Once she practised and learned the routine, the fear would go away, and her confidence in herself would grow. She could add another skill to those she had already. That's simply the way it works – *for all of us*. Because we are all human, we share the same feelings. Fear is one of them.

Many stories similar to Louise's appear in newspapers, magazines, books and on television. Until you are in touch with the Fear Truths, you will hear about and read and see these stories, and not notice how the same truths apply to everyone.

You may never connect the lives of others, especially of celebrities, to your own life. You may think they are lucky because they aren't afraid to perform in public. *Not so!* They had to push through huge amounts of fear to get where they are today... and they are still pushing.

Those who have dealt with fear well all their lives seem to have known somehow, in their heads or their hearts, the message in this book: You must feel the fear... and do it anyway.

A friend of mine, a wealthy, self-made man who let nothing stop him along the way, thought about the title of my book one day. He nodded, and said, 'Yes, I guess that is the way I've always lived my life, without realising that's what I've been doing. I can't remember not being afraid. But I never thought that fear would prevent me from taking the risks I needed to take to get what I wanted. I just went ahead and did what I had to do to make my ideas work – despite the fear.'

If you have not dealt with fear well, you probably never learned the Fear Truths. You saw fear as a signal to back off rather than as a green light to move ahead. You have tended to play those WHEN/THEN games that I wrote about earlier. All you have to do to find a way out of the prison you have made for yourself is to retrain your thinking.

A first step in retraining your thinking is to say the Fear Truths at least ten times a day for the next month. As you will soon find out, repeating the Fear Truths is a part of retraining faulty thinking. *Knowing* the Fear Truths is not enough. You have to keep saying them to yourself until they become a part of your being. You need to do this until you start to change your behaviour and move *towards* your goals, rather than away from them. There will be more later about why repeating things is important. For now, just trust me and repeat the Fear Truths over and over again.

Before you begin, however, I'd like to add one very important Fear Truth to the list. You might already have been asking yourself, 'Why should I put myself through all the pain that comes with taking risks? Why don't I just go

on living my life the way I've been living it?'
You might find my answer to that question
surprising. It is:

TRUTH 5

**Pushing through fear is less frightening
than living with the constant fear that
comes from a feeling of helplessness.**

Read it again. I know it's hard to take in at first.
It says that no matter how secure any of us feel
in the little shelter we have built for ourselves,
we live – whether we know it consciously or
not – with the fear that something awful will
eventually happen.

The more helpless we feel, the deeper is
the feeling of dread that comes with knowing
there are events in life over which we have
no control – such as the death of a spouse or
the loss of a job. We find ourselves worrying
madly about possible disasters. 'What if...?'
Fear completely fills our lives. That is the
mystery of Fear Truth 5: people who refuse to
take risks live with a feeling of dread that is far
deeper than the fear they would feel if they
took the risks that would make them feel less
helpless. But they don't know it!

Five Truths about Fear

1. The fear will never go away as long as I continue to grow.
2. The only way to get rid of the fear of doing something is to go out... and do it.
3. The only way to feel better about myself is to go out... and do it.
4. I am going to feel fear whenever I do something new, but so will everyone else.
5. Pushing through fear is less frightening than living with the basic fear that comes from a feeling of helplessness.

Chapter 3

From Pain to Power

The last chapter revealed an important truth:

**Everybody feels fear when
dealing with
something totally new in life,
yet many people are out there 'doing it'
anyway.
This must mean that
*fear is not the problem.***

Obviously, the real issue has nothing to do with the fear itself, but rather how we *hold* the fear. For some, the fear is totally not a problem. They hold their fear from a place of power (their fear gives them choice, energy and action). For others, it creates a state of shut down and they hold their fear from a place of pain (their fear makes them feel helpless, depressed and stuck).

The chart on the next page shows this idea.

```
┌─────────────────────────────────────────────┐
│             HOW WE HOLD FEAR                  │
│                                               │
│    Pain                          Power        │
│  ───────────────────────────────────────      │
│     │                              │          │
│  Helplessness ................... Choice       │
│     │                              │          │
│  Depression  ................... Excitement    │
│     │                              │          │
│  Paralysis  ................... Action         │
│     │                              │          │
└─────────────────────────────────────────────┘
```

From this it can be seen that the secret to handling fear is to move yourself from a place of pain to a place of power. The fact that you have the fear then stops being a problem.

Let's talk about the word 'power'. Some people say that they do not like the idea of power and want no part of it. It is true that the word 'power' often suggests control over others, and such power is often used badly.

The kind of power I am talking about is different. In fact, it makes you *less* likely to try to control those around you, and certainly more loving. I am talking about *within you, power within the self*. This means:

- Power over your understanding of the world.
- Power over how you react to events in your life.

- Power to do what is needed for your self-growth.
- Power to create joy and happiness in your life.
- Power to act.
- Power to love.

This kind of power has nothing to do with anyone else. It is not being completely hung up on yourself. Instead, it is a healthy self-love. In fact, people who are completely hung up on themselves have absolutely no feeling of power – so they have a strong need to control those around them. Their lack of power leaves them constantly in a state of fear, because their lives depend on the outside world. No one is more unloving than a person who can't sense his or her own power. Such people spend their lives trying to pull power out of everyone else. Their need creates all sorts of crafty behaviour.

The kind of power I'm talking about leaves you free, since you don't expect the rest of the world to fill you with power. It's not being able to get someone else to do what you want them to do. It's being able to get yourself to do what you want to do. If you do not have this kind of power, you lose your sense of peace. You are in a very unsafe place.

Now that I've explained the kind of power I'm talking about, let's explore how to use the Pain-to-Power idea in daily life.

The first step is to create a Pain-to-Power Chart, as follows:

PAIN-TO-POWER CHART

Pain ➝ ➝ ➝ ➝ ➝ ➝ ➝ Power

As we look at the Pain-to-Power chart, most of us can place ourselves somewhere in the middle of it. We're not totally held back by our fears, but we're not feeling a great sense of power and excitement either. We are not moving quickly towards our goals. We seem to be taking the hardest route over the mountain carrying two suitcases and a watermelon, rather than flying on the wings of eagles. As an ancient wise man once said, 'The pathway is smooth. Why do you throw rocks before you?'

Using the Pain-to-Power Chart to help, you can begin to clear the rocks in front of you. These steps will help you clear the way:

1. Draw a large copy of the Pain-to-Power Chart and stick it on your wall. Just the simple act of making it larger will make you

feel a little more powerful. You are already taking action! Remember that much of the trick of moving from pain to power is taking action – action is very powerful! Once the chart is on your wall it will always remind you of where you want to go in life – from pain to power. Awareness, knowledge, is half the battle. Having the chart on your wall will also help you to keep moving forward.

2. Put a pin at the place on the chart where you see yourself at this moment in your life.

Are you in the middle, where you sometimes feel depressed and stuck, and at other times more in control?

Or do you find yourself on the far left side, where there is little you are able to do to pull yourself out of the rut?

Or perhaps you are already on the right side, where you feel you are really moving ahead with your life, with only a few areas that need to be worked on.

I doubt that anyone reading this book has reached their goal of gaining total power over the self. Even the Buddhas don't have power over their selves all the time! There are always new events that challenge a sense of personal power.

3. Each day look at the chart and ask yourself, 'Do I see myself at the same place, or have I moved?' Move the pin if you have moved.

4. If you keep in mind the way you want to go, it will help you make choices about what you are doing in your life. Before you take any action in life, ask yourself: 'Is this action moving me to a more powerful place?' If it isn't, think again about doing it. *A word of warning* – if you go ahead anyway, knowing the action will keep you in a place of pain, don't get angry with yourself about it. Use your mistakes to learn more about yourself.

5. Make your use of the chart fun. Having it as a game keeps you relaxed about how you are getting on. If you have children, they can create their own charts, and you can make a family game out of the fun of growing.

6. You might want to make different charts for different areas of your life. To be really powerful, you need to be in charge of all aspects of your life – your work, relationships, home, body, and so on. Often people are very powerful in some parts of their lives and very weak in others. For example, I am very powerful in terms of my career, but need to work on the area of exercise.

To help you on your Pain-to-Power path, it's important that you begin to develop Pain-to-Power words. The way you use words has a huge impact on the quality of your life. Certain words make you weaker; others make you powerful. Choose to move to Pain-to-Power Words as follows:

PAIN-TO-POWER VOCABULARY

Pain ➤ ➤ ➤ ➤ ➤ Power	
I can't	I won't
I should	I could
It's not may fault	I'm totally responsible
It's a problem	It's an opportunity
I'm never satisfied	I want to learn and grow
Life's a struggle	Life's an adventure
I hope	I know
If only	Next time
What will I do?	I know I can handle it
It's terrible	It's a learning experience

- 'I can't' suggests you have no control over your life, but '*I won't*' puts an issue in the area of choice. From this moment on, stop saying, 'I can't'. Your inner self is called the subconscious. It is a part of your mind of which you are not directly aware.

31

If you say, or think, 'I can't', your subconscious really believes you and stores the message: Weak... weak... weak. You might be saying 'I can't' simply to get out of a dinner date with a friend. You might say, 'I can't come to dinner tonight, I have to prepare for tomorrow's meeting' – but your subconscious is storing up, 'He's weak!' The truth is 'I *can* come to dinner, but I *am choosing* to do something that is more important at the moment.' But the subconscious can't tell the difference and is still storing 'weak'.

Although you may want to be more polite to your friend than to tell the exact truth, as written above, you can still stay away from the words 'I can't'. 'I'd love to come to dinner, but I have a meeting tomorrow that's important to me. I'll feel better walking in totally prepared.' Those words have truth and power, and show respect to your friend. The subconscious hears you saying what is important to you clearly and it hears you making a choice that serves your own growth.

- 'I should' is another pain, rather than power, word. It, too, suggests that you have no choices in life. '*I could*' is more powerful. 'I could visit my mother, but I'm choosing to go to the cinema today.' This puts things in the area of choice instead of duty. 'I can visit my mother or I can go to the cinema. I think I'll choose my mother today.' 'Shoulds' bring on guilt and upset. They make you suffer rather than feel powerful. Your power is taken away every time you say the words 'I should'.

- 'It's not my fault' is another bad one. Once again, you look helpless. It's better to take charge of whatever happens to you in life, rather than always be the victim. 'It's not my fault I got sick.' 'It's not my fault I lost the job.' If you are willing to accept that you played a part in whatever happened, then you might see what you can change in the future.

- 'It's a problem' is another phrase that takes away your power. It's heavy and unhelpful. '*It's an opportunity*' looks forward and can lead you to growth. Each time you can see the opportunity in life's difficulties, you can handle tricky issues in a rewarding way. Each time you have the opportunity to stretch your ability to deal with the world, the more powerful you become.

- 'I hope' are also the words of a victim. '*I know*' has far more power. 'I hope I will get a job.' 'I know I will get a job.' What a difference! The first sets you up for worry and sleepless nights. The second has peace and calm about it.

- 'If only' is boring. You can hear the whine behind it. *'Next time'* implies that you have learned from what happened and will put the learning to use another time. For example, 'If only I hadn't said that to Tom' can be said as, 'I've learned Tom can get upset about this issue. Next time, *I'll* be more careful.'

- 'What will I do?' Again you can hear the whine and the fear in these words. You, like everyone else, have great sources of power within that you haven't used before. It would help you to say to yourself, *'I know I'll handle it.* I have nothing to worry about.' Instead of 'I've lost my job! What will I do?' Try 'I've lost my job. I know I'll handle it.'

- 'It's terrible' is used a lot at the wrong moments. For example, 'I lost my wallet. Isn't that terrible?' What's so terrible about losing a wallet? It's certainly a nuisance; it's hardly terrible. 'I gained two pounds. Isn't that terrible?' It's hardly terrible to gain two pounds. Yet that's the way we talk about small things in our lives. And our subconscious is storing it up, Disaster... disaster... disaster. Replace 'It's terrible' with *'It's an opportunity to learn'*.

You get the idea. Begin taking out the terribles, can'ts, problems, struggles, and so on from the words you use. You might think that these changes of words are a small matter, but I assure you they are not. Not only does your sense of yourself change with more powerful words, so also does your presence in the world. People who show an inner strength are treated differently from those who come across as weak. The more power you show when you speak, the more you will be a force in the world around you.

Your comfort zone

As you begin to look at the words you use, you can also bring more power into your life by *expanding your comfort zone*. What does that mean?

Most of us live within a zone that feels right. We don't feel comfortable outside of that zone. For example, we might spend £50 on a pair of shoes, but £75 would make us nervous. We might be willing to start friendships with people at the office who are at our level in the company. But we would feel nervous if we became friends with one of the managers or bosses. We might go to the local cafe when eating alone, but would feel really awkward in a posh restaurant on our own. We might ask for a £3,000 rise, but £5,000 would make us feel tense. We may charge £15 an hour for our work, but we don't feel we are worth £20. And so on.

For each one of us that zone of comfort is different. But whether we realise it or not, all of us make decisions based on the limits of that comfort zone.

I suggest that each day you do something that makes your comfort zone larger.

- Phone someone you are frightened to phone.
- Buy a pair of shoes that costs more than you would ever have paid in the past.
- Ask for something you want that you have been too frightened to ask for before.

Even if it doesn't work out the way you wanted it to, at least you've tried. Watch what starts to happen when you expand your comfort zone:

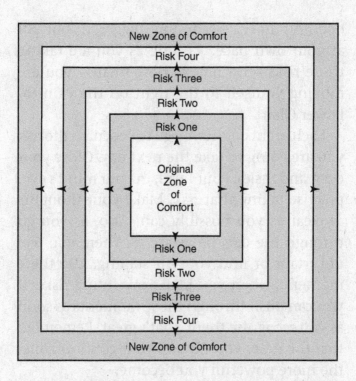

New Zone of Comfort
Risk Four
Risk Three
Risk Two
Risk One

Original
Zone
of
Comfort

Risk One
Risk Two
Risk Three
Risk Four
New Zone of Comfort

As the drawing shows, with each risk you take and each time you move out of what feels comfortable, you become more powerful. As your power builds, so does your confidence, so that stretching your comfort zone becomes easier and easier, despite any fear you may feel. The size of the risks you take also expands. In the beginning you might sign up for one evening course after being out of school for fifteen years. In the end you might sign up for your graduate degree. You will be expanding…

opening up... becoming bigger... but all at your own pace. As long as you are taking those risks – no matter how small – you are moving yourself to the right on the Pain-to-Power Chart.

Each night before you go to bed, plan the risk you are going to take the next day. Close your eyes, and inside your head, in your mind's eye, practise taking that risk. Make your thoughts as clear as you possibly can. Also, as you go through the day, be aware of where you feel uncertain or find yourself stalling. Use these moments when you plan your future risks. If you can push through those moments as soon as you recognise them, that's great. Remember that the more you expand your comfort zone, the more powerful you become.

Please note: *The risks I am talking about do not include dangerous acts, such as speeding in a car, or taking drugs. Nor do they include risks that ignore the rights of other people, such as making a pass at someone's partner or, for that matter, robbing a bank. Not only could you end up unpopular, dead or in prison, but also you would be moving yourself far to the left side of the Pain-to-Power Chart. These kinds of acts are not empowering, because they do not have any respect or love – for yourself or others – behind them. Without those qualities, it is impossible to build your sense of self-worth. So your ability to handle fear would be greatly reduced.*

So take only those risks each day that build your sense of self-esteem. These are the risks that stretch your ability to deal with your fears. Expand! Expand! Expand!

Whether it feels like it or not, you already have more power than you could ever have dreamed of. We all have. When I speak of going from pain to power, I am not talking about pulling the power in from any outside source. Inside of you, just waiting to come out, is a vast source of energy, which is more than enough for you to create a joyful and satisfying life. It isn't magic. It is only a matter of tapping into the energy already there, though you are not aware of it.

You are innately designed to use your personal power ....

Chapter 4

Whether You Want It
or Not … It's Yours

Are you a 'victim', or are you taking charge of your life? So many of us *think* we are taking charge of our own lives when we simply are not. It's sometimes hard to see that we think of ourselves as victims. And that thinking takes many forms. Once you understand the ideas in this chapter you will better understand the forces involved in handling fear.

The idea of taking charge of your own life is probably not totally new to you. For years you have been swamped with the message: Take charge of your own life.

But I am sure that most of us do not really understand what that means.

To most *independent* people, it has meant that we should get a job, earn enough money to support ourselves and not depend on anyone else for our livings. That may or may not be part of the meaning. (I know many *dependent* people who understand the secret of taking charge of their experience of life.) But having a job, money and being independent certainly doesn't hit the heart of the issue of taking charge. It is a much bigger issue than that, and yet it is more invisible. Let's look at a few examples.

Edward is very wealthy, clever and hard-working, yet he lives in a constant state of anxiety. When I suggested that he get some help to improve his mental state, he replied that if the people in his life would change, everything would be fine. If only his wife would be more loving, if only his boss wasn't always leaning on him, and if only his son would stop taking drugs – then he'd be fine. He feels there is no reason for him to get help – it's all *their* fault. Is he taking charge of his experience of life? Absolutely not!

You would think that Mara has a lovely life ... She has a great job, lives in a lovely apartment, has many friends and lovers. Yet she complains all the time about her ex-husband – he is making her life miserable, he has always been unfair to her, he never pays child support. Also, her son is turning against her and says she is selfish ... and on ... and on ... and on. Is she taking charge of her experience of life? Absolutely not!

I know many single or divorced people who are always complaining about their ex-husbands or their ex-wives, their bosses, their loneliness, their problems with dating, and so on. I know many married people who are constantly complaining about their children, their lack of money, their poor relationship with their spouses, and so on. Are any of them really taking charge of their experience of life? Not at all!

They are all, in some way, playing the role of victim. They have given their power to someone or something else. Keep in mind that when you give away your power, you move farther and farther to the left side of the Pain-to-Power Chart, and as a result you become frozen in your attempts to deal with fear.

You are also playing the role of victim on a more obvious level:

- If you're in a job you hate.
- If you're single and you want to be married.
- If you're in a rotten relationship and want to get out.
- If your daughter is making you grey before your time.
- If, in general, nothing seems to go the way you want it to go.

No wonder you feel fearful – victims are powerless!

The truth is you really are in control – in total control. For some reason:

- You are consciously or unconsciously choosing to be in that awful job.
- You are choosing to hate the single life.
- You are choosing to stay in a destructive relationship.
- You are choosing to let your daughter drive you crazy.
- You are choosing to spoil anything good in your life.
- You are choosing whatever else makes you feel like a victim.

I know it is difficult to accept the fact that you are the cause of the feelings that take away your joy in life. It is very upsetting when you begin to see yourself as your own worst enemy. On the other hand, *this realisation is your biggest blessing*. If you know you can create your own misery, then you must also be able to create your own joy.

As you read the following seven definitions of taking charge, keep in mind that whenever you are not taking charge, you put yourself in a place of pain, and you will reduce your ability to handle the fear in your life.

1. *Taking charge means never blaming anyone else for anything you are being, doing, having or feeling.* 'Never?' you say. 'But this time it really is his fault.' (Or her fault, or the boss's fault, or my son's fault, or the economy's fault, or my mother's fault, or my father's fault, or my friend's fault!) 'Really, it is!' If I missed anyone or anything, just add it to the list. Until you fully understand that *you*, and no one else, create what goes on in your head, you will never be in control of your life.

2. *Taking charge means not blaming yourself.* I know this sounds at odds with the idea of taking charge, but it is not. *Anything* that takes away your power or your pleasure makes you a victim. Don't make yourself a victim of yourself!

   For some, not blaming themselves is more difficult than not blaming others. Once you become aware that you have created so much of your unhappiness, you might tend to punish yourself and put yourself down. 'There I am messing up my life again. I'm hopeless. When will I ever learn?'

This, again, is not taking charge of your experience of life. It is important to understand that you have always done the best you possibly could, given the person you were at any particular time. Now that you are learning a new way of thinking, you can begin to see things differently and perhaps change many of your actions.

There is absolutely no need to be upset with your past, present or future behaviour. It is all simply part of the learning process – the process of moving yourself from pain to power. And it takes time. You must be patient with yourself. There is *never* any need to blame yourself. Nothing is your 'fault'. Yes, you cause your unhappiness, but this is no reason to cast blame. You're simply on the path towards a fuller enjoyment of life, and it is a lengthy process of trial and error.

3. *Taking charge means being aware of where and when you are* not *taking charge so that you can eventually change.* It took years before I realised that I played the victim role most often with the men in my life. I remember many evenings of complaining for hours with my girlfriends about the pain the men in my life were causing me.

Those jerks, as I so smugly called them, were always doing something to take away my happiness. One was always late. One was mean with money. One didn't make enough money. One loved to play golf too much. One wouldn't get a divorce, and so on.

I was able to build up incredible anger about them. I was on the phone for hours and hours yelling, 'Would you believe he actually...' Naturally, my loyal friends shared my drama because I shared their upsets about their men. It was a Moan and Groan Club. We never seemed to tire of each other's stories. No wonder – we fed each other the misery we were clearly enjoying, and we always got to be right! The result was that we didn't have to create our own happiness – we could simply blame men for not giving it to us.

During this time I was certain I was taking charge of my life. Just like my friend Mara, I was earning good money. I had a great flat. I was totally independent. But I *wasn't* taking charge of my life. I was still expecting the men in my life to 'make me happy'. I finally learned there is really only one person in the world who can make me happy, and that is *me*! And only after learning that was I able, for the first time, to have a wonderfully caring relationship.

Now I know that when I am angry at my husband, I simply have to ask myself, 'What am I not doing in my life, that I could be doing, that I am blaming him for not doing for me?' (Read that one again!) I am now quickly able to understand what it is. Either I'm worrying too much about money, or I'm feeling shaky, or I'm not doing enough for myself, or I'm expecting him to make 'all better' something I'm not dealing with.

Once I realise what I am doing, I can begin to correct it. As I correct what needs to be sorted out in my life, all my anger towards others goes away. My daughter, Leslie, recently told me how fantastic my marriage is. 'Yes,' I said, 'it's amazing how perfect Mark becomes when I stop expecting him to deal with my life!'

This is not to say that you can't have your basic needs met by your partner – the need to be supported in your growth, the need to be looked after at times, the need to know your partner cares for you. But when you are not dealing with your life, no amount of caring is enough. You want the man in your life to do everything. He could stand on his head for you, as some of the men in my life tried to do, but it is never enough.

One sign that you are truly taking charge is when you feel little or no anger towards your partner. You realise that you chose to be angry in the past and you are now choosing to change that in the future. Nothing is the other's fault. She (or he) is doing the best she (or he) can given her (or his) level of growth. Anger is a sign that you are not taking charge.

Your relationship with a partner is only one area where you can give away your power. It is important to look at all other areas of your life as well, to see where you are not taking charge. Look for any of the following signs:

- Anger.
- Impatience.
- Upset.
- Feeling gloomy.
- Blaming others.
- Tiredness.
- Pain.
- Trying to control others.
- Finding it hard to focus.
- Worrying obsessively.
- Self-pity.

- Addictions.
- Envy.
- Judging other people.
- Feeling helpless.
- Feeling disappointed.
- Always waiting for something to happen.
- Jealousy.

This is not a complete list, but you should get the idea. Whenever you feel any of these, work out what you are *not* doing in your life that is causing the sign. You will be surprised how easy it is to find the area where you are not taking charge of your life.

4. *Taking charge means handling the Chatterbox.* This is the little voice inside, the voice that tries to drive you crazy – and often succeeds! I'll bet some of you don't even know it's there. I was shocked when I became aware of it. But I promise you it holds the key to all your fears. It's the voice that signals doom, loss and losing. We're so used to it being there that we often don't even notice it is talking to us. If you are not aware of your Chatterbox, it sounds something like this:

If I call him maybe he'll think I'm too pushy. But maybe if I don't call him, he'll think I'm not interested. But if I call him and his message machine is on, I'll wonder where he is. And that will ruin my whole evening because I'll know he is out with another woman. But if I don't call I'll wonder anyway. Maybe I shouldn't go out tonight. He might call and then he'll think I'm out with someone else. And he'll think I don't care. But if I call he'll really know I'm interested and he'll probably start backing away from me. I wonder why he hasn't called. Maybe I was too cool this afternoon when I bumped into him at lunch. Maybe I should have been warmer. I wonder if it was because he heard I went out with Allen the other night. Well, I don't think he should expect me to sit at home every night and wait for him to call. He has a lot of nerve if he expects that. The next time I see him I'll ask him why he hasn't called. We were supposed to go to the movies this week, and he didn't even remember.

Or this:

I'm really angry at my boss for not asking me to the meeting this morning. He really doesn't value all the work I do for him. The others spend their days lazing about and they get to go to the meeting. Maybe I'll try lazing about and see if he likes that better. It really doesn't pay to give your all to a job. You never get rewarded for all the hard work. It just pays to be a big crafty controller, like all the rest. An honest hard worker is just not valued any more. I'll show him. I'll look around for another job. But the job market is so bad right now, I'd never find anything. I wish I had finished my degree – then I'd have a better chance. I'm really stuck here ... no one is hiring people over forty any more. It's all in who you know. If my parents had had money, I would have been friends with people who have some power. I really feel used. I can't believe they left me out of the meeting. Who does he think he is? This kind of thing always happens to me ...

No wonder so many of us hate being alone, and can't be in a room without turning on the radio or television for company. Anything to escape such a mad nagging voice! But I assure you that this mad nagging is a stage in the growth process. We are all victims of our Chatterboxes at some point in our lives.

Now that you know it exists, you will also notice that you can't seem to turn it off – at least not yet. The good news is that there are very useful ways to get rid of this kind of harmful thinking, which will be set out later in this book.

For now, simply notice that your Chatterbox is making you a victim, and commit yourself to turning it into a loving voice. You don't have to live with your enemies, even if they are within yourself. By the way, once you get rid of the harmful thinking your Chatterbox brings, you will really begin to enjoy being alone.

5. *Taking charge means being aware of the rewards that keep you stuck where you are.* Rewards explain why we choose to carry on with things we don't want in our lives. Once you understand rewards, your behaviour will make much more sense to you.

6. *Taking charge means working out what you want in life and acting on it.* Set your goals – then go out and work towards them.

   Work out what kind of space you would like to live in... then create it. It doesn't take a lot of money to create a peaceful, loving home for yourself.

   Look around and see who you would love to have in your circle of friends... then pick up the phone and make plans to get together. Don't sit around waiting for them to call you.

Check out your body. Decide what you need to do to create what looks and feels healthy... then make it happen.

Most of us do not shape our lives. We accept what comes our way... then we moan about it. Many of us spend our lives waiting – waiting for the perfect mate, waiting for the perfect job, waiting for perfect friends to come along. There is no need to wait for anyone to give you anything in your life. You have the power to create what you need. Given commitment, clear goals and action, it's just a matter of time.

7. *Taking charge means being aware of the many choices you have about any issue.* As you go through each day, it is important to realise that at every moment you are choosing the way you feel. When a difficult issue comes into your life, it is possible to say to your mind, 'Okay, choose'. Are you going to make yourself miserable or content? The choice is certainly yours. Pick the one that adds most to your growth and your sense of being alive. The point is simply to begin. You will start to feel better immediately.

Seven Ways to Reclaim Your Power

1. Don't blame forces outside yourself for your bad feelings about life. Nothing outside yourself can control your thinking or your actions.

2. Don't blame yourself for not being in control. You are doing the best you can, and you are on the way to taking back your power.

3. Be aware of when and where you are playing the role of victim. Learn the signs that tell you that you are not taking charge of what you are being, having, doing or feeling.

4. Get to know your biggest enemy – your Chatterbox. Use the exercises in this book to replace it with a loving internal friend.

5. Look for the rewards that keep you stuck where you are. Strangely, once you find them, you will probably be able quickly to become 'unstuck'.

6. Decide what you want in life and act on it. Stop waiting for someone to give it to you. You'll be waiting a long time.

7. Be aware of the many choices you have – in both actions and feelings – in any event that comes your way. Choose the path that adds to your growth and makes you feel at peace with yourself and others.

Chapter 5

How to Make a No-Lose Decision

We all have a big fear of making decisions. It keeps us from moving ahead with our lives The problem is that we have been taught, 'Be careful! You might make the wrong decision!' A *wrong* decision! Just the sound of that can bring terror to our hearts. We are afraid that the wrong decision will make us lose something – money, friends, lovers, status or whatever the *right* decision is supposed to bring us.

Our panic over making mistakes is closely linked to this. For some reason we feel we should be perfect, and forget that we *learn* from our mistakes. Our need to be perfect and our need to control the outcome of events work together to frighten us when we think about making a change or trying something new.

If you fear making decisions, I am going to show you that you need not worry. There really is nothing to lose, only something to gain, whatever the choices you make or actions you take in life. As I said earlier, *all you have to do to change your world is change the way you think about it*. This idea works beautifully here. You can actually shift your thinking in such a way as to make a wrong decision or mistake *impossible*. Let's begin with making decisions.

Suppose you are at a Choice Point in life. If you are like most of us, you have been taught to use the No-Win Model as you think about the decision to be made. The model looks like this:

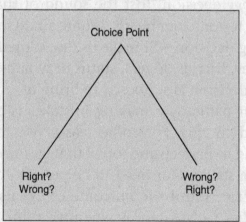

NO-WIN MODEL

Choice Point

Right?
Wrong?

Wrong?
Right?

Your heart feels heavy about the choice you have to make.

You feel somewhat stuck as you think about the results in life-and-death terms. You stand on the edge of the decision, complaining and worrying: 'Should I do this or should I do that? What if I go this way and that happens? What if it doesn't work out the way I plan? What if…' The 'what ifs' are out in full force. The Chatterbox inside you is hard at work. You look at the unknown and try to predict the future. You try to take control of outside forces. Neither is possible. At this point you might notice that you are driving yourself crazy.

After the decision is made, the No-Win Model makes you constantly review the issue, hoping you didn't make a mistake. You keep looking back and telling yourself off by saying 'If only I had…' You waste energy and you also make yourself miserable.

You feel better if the outcome is as you hoped it would be – *but* only for a little while. Soon you are worrying that the outcome might change and that it might *in the end* prove to be the wrong decision.

Worse still, you are already worrying about the next decision you have to make, because you will have to go through the whole painful process once again. Does this sound like you?

Crazy, isn't it! Clearly, this is a no-win decision. But there is another way – the No-Lose Model.

Go back and stand at the Choice Point again. This time, the choice looks like this:

NO-LOSE MODEL

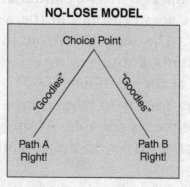

Notice that what lies ahead are simply two paths – A and B – *both of which are right!* Each path has nothing but 'goodies' along the way. You are clearly facing a no-lose choice. And what are these goodies? They are opportunities to live life in a new way, to learn and grow. They are opportunities to find out who you are, and who you would really like to be, and what you would like to do in this life. Each path is full of opportunities – *whatever the outcome.*

'What?' you ask. '*Whatever the outcome?*' Up to this point you may have been willing to go along with me, but those three words are making you a little unsure, if not downright scared. 'What if…' comes up again in your thinking. Let me answer your 'what ifs' with an example.

Imagine you are faced with the choice of staying with your present job or taking a new one that has opened up for you. If you stand at the No-Win Choice Point, your Chatterbox takes over and craziness begins:

> 'If I stay here, I might be missing a very good chance to move ahead. But if I go, maybe I won't be able to cope with my new job. What if I get fired from the new job, and then I have nothing? I really like it here. I'll have more opportunity to move ahead in the new job. Maybe they'll promote me and I'll be making more money. But what if I regret leaving? What if… ? Oh, I don't know what to do! I could ruin my whole life if I make the wrong decision!'

If you stand at the No-Lose Choice Point, your 'fearless' self takes over:

> 'Isn't it fantastic! I've been offered a new job. If I take it, I'll have an opportunity to meet new people, to learn new ways of doing things, to find out about an entirely

different work place and to broaden my experience. If something happens and it doesn't work out, I know I'll handle it.

Even though the job market is difficult right now, I know somehow I'll find another job if I need one. Even that will be an interesting adventure, since I'll learn to deal with losing a job and learn to solve the problems that might come up if I am unemployed.

If I stay, I have an opportunity to build on the contacts I have made here. I really feel better about myself because I have been offered the other job. So if I stay, perhaps I'll ask for a promotion. If for some reason it doesn't work out here, there will be other opportunities to pursue. It's all an adventure, no matter which way I turn.'

I really do know people who think this way – and their approach to life is a joy to be around. They truly live in a no-lose world.

It's interesting to me that when I present the No-Lose Model to my students, they resist it strongly at first. 'Oh, come on, you're not being realistic.' As I said earlier, we have been taught to believe that no action is realistic and safe, and taking action is unrealistic and risky.

When I question my students, they can't find more belief in the No-Win Model than in the No-Lose Model. Yet the No-Lose Model can move us from a place of pain to one of power, which is in the end our goal as we learn to deal with fear.

Another point is that *it feels better to come from a no-lose position*. Why resist coming from a no-lose position? Why continue to feel pain, to feel stuck and depressed? Yet we go on doing it until we take into our being another way of seeing the world. Then we can slowly begin to change the no-win thinking that has kept us feeling that we are victims.

A big factor in your accepting the No-Lose Model is the way you think about outcomes and opportunities. It might be hard for you to accept that losing a job is a no-lose event. Opportunities in life are thought of as relating to money, status and the visible signs of success. I'm asking you to think of opportunity in an entirely different way. The purpose of this book is to help you handle fear in a way that allows you to fulfill your goals in life. Every time you face something that forces you to 'handle it,' your self-esteem is raised a long way. You learn to trust that you will survive, no matter what happens. And in this way your fears fade away.

The knowledge that you can handle anything that comes your way is the key to allowing yourself to take healthy, life-affirming risks.

You've learned that there really are no right or wrong decisions when using the No-Lose Model. From there are steps you can take to improve your awareness of the options on offer to you. This awareness will improve the chances of the outcome being what you want, and will give you greater peace of mind. I suggest that the following steps are taken when you face a major decision, and after you've made such a decision.

Before Making a Decision

1. *Focus immediately on the No-Lose Model.* Promise yourself, 'I can't lose – whatever the outcome of the decision I make. The world is a place for opportunity, and I look forward to the opportunities for learning and growing that either pathway gives me.' Push away thoughts of what you can lose and allow only thoughts of what can be gained.
2. *Do your homework.* There is much to learn about the options on offer to you. It is helpful to talk to as many people as will listen. Don't be afraid to go to professionals who have

experience of the decision to be made. A few might be too busy to talk to you, but most will be happy to help. In fact, they will be pleased that you came to them for advice.

Look for advice from other sources as well. Talk to people at parties, in the hairdresser's, the doctor's office, the school playground, or wherever. People you meet in unlikely places can come up with ideas that will help you in ways you never could have imagined. Or they might tell you something useful learned from their own experiences.

It is important that you talk to the right people. The right people are those who support your learning and growing. People who constantly put down the options open to you, are the wrong people to talk to. Politely say thank you and go on to someone else.

Also, be sure to talk about your plans even if you fear that if they don't work out you'll look like a failure. Don't be proud. By not finding out as much as you can, you are cutting off valuable sources of advice that might greatly help you. Remember:

You're not a failure if you don't make it – you're a success because you try.

3. *Decide what is important to you.* This will need some deep thought. Give yourself time to really think about what you want out of life. This is a difficult thing for most of us to work out, since we are trained at an early age to do what other people want us to do. We have forgotten those things that really make us happy. To make it easier, ask yourself which pathway is more in line with your overall goals in life – at the present time.

It is important to remember that goals constantly change as you go through life, and you have to keep checking them. The decision you make today might not be the decision you would make five years from now. If you are having trouble making your overall goals clear, don't worry. It may take many more decisions and many more experiences after you have made different choices to find out what is important to you. At least you are now paying attention to who you are. Allow yourself confusion as you search. It is through confusion that you finally come to see clearly.

4. *Trust your instinct, your gut feeling.* You might find it hard to find out what is important to you by just thinking. Sometimes your body

gives some good signs about which way you should go. Even after you've thought hard, talked to many people and come up with a clear choice, it is possible that your instinct is telling you to go with the other choice. Don't be afraid to trust your instinct. Very often your subconscious mind sends messages as to which choice is better. As you start paying attention to your instinct, your impulses, your gut feeling, you will be surprised at the good advice you are giving yourself.

5. *Relax.* We live in a world where most people take themselves and their decisions very seriously. I have news for you. Nothing is *that* important. Honestly! If as a result of a decision you make, you lose some money, no problem – you learn to deal with losing money. If you lose a lover, no problem – you find another one. If you choose to divorce, no problem – you learn to handle living on your own. If you choose to marry, no problem – you learn to handle a new kind of sharing.

After Making a Decision

1. *Throw away your picture.* We all create visions, or pictures, of what we would like to happen

after a decision is made. The picture in our mind's eye might have helped us make a decision. But once the decision is made, let the picture go. Since you can't control the future, the picture can create upset if things don't work out that way. Feeling disappointed may make you miss the good that can come out of every place in which you find yourself. Don't forget to look for the upside. If you focus on 'the way it's supposed to be', you might miss the opportunity to enjoy the way it is. Or you might miss the opportunity for it to be wonderful in a different way from what your picture.

2. *Accept that your decisions are yours and no-one else's. Accept that you are responsible for your decisions.* This is a tough one! We all tend to look for someone to blame if things don't work out to our liking. I really hated my financial advisor when shares he suggested I buy went down in price instead of up. It was a great effort to admit to myself, 'I made the decision to buy. No one made me do that.' I made a fuss until I created an 'opportunity' from my unlucky decision.

What did I learn? A lot! I learned I had to find out more about shares and the stock market, instead of relying on my advisor's opinion. I learned that I was terribly worried about money, and had to work on that. I learned that I could lose money in the stock market, and yet life went on just as it did before.

I learned that, if in the future I lost money in the stock market, it wouldn't be such a big deal. I learned that shares can go up again, as mine did eight months later. When looked at that way, it wasn't a bad decision after all. When you can find the *opportunity* in any decision, it is much easier to accept the *responsibility* for making the decision.

When you take charge and take responsibility for your decisions, you become a lot less angry at the world, and, most important, a lot less angry at yourself!

3. *Don't protect, correct.* It is most important to commit yourself to any decision you make and give it all you've got. But if it doesn't work out, *change it!* Many of us are so keen to make the right decision that we stick to it, even if we find we don't like the path we have chosen. This is just crazy. There is great value in learning you *don't* like something. Then it is simply a matter of changing your path.

There are those, of course, who flit from one path to another, using 'change it' as an excuse not to commit to a decision. I'm not talking about that, and you'll know the difference within yourself. If you've truly committed yourself to something, if you've given it everything you've got, and then decided that it is not for you – move on to something else.

When you decide to change paths, you will often face an attack from those around you. 'What do you mean you want to change your career? You've invested five years in building up your dental practice! All that time and money down the drain!' Explain to them that none of it has been a waste. At one time it was the right thing for you to do. Much was learned and much experience was gained. But now it simply doesn't feel right any more – it's time to change.

I know many people who stay locked in jobs or relationships that no longer work for them because they've put so much into it and it would be a shame not to carry on. How absurd! Why put more in, if it's no longer paying off? Remember – the quality of your life is at stake!

In his book *Actualizations*, Stewart Emery presents a useful model for changing your direction in life. He learned it while sitting on the flight deck of a plane on the way to Hawaii. He noticed a control panel, which the pilot told him was 'the inertial guidance system'. The purpose of the system was to get the plane within one thousand yards of the runway in Hawaii within five minutes of the planned arrival time. Each time the plane strayed off course, the system corrected it. The pilot explained that they would arrive in Hawaii on time in spite of *'having been in error 90 per cent of the time'*.

Emery explains: 'So the path from here to where we want to be starts with an error, which we correct, which becomes the next error, which we correct and that becomes the next error, which we correct. So the only time we are truly on course is that moment in the zigzag when we actually cross the true path.' From this example, we see that the trick in life is not to worry about making a wrong decision; *it's learning when to correct*! My idea of the model looks like this:

OFF-COURSE MODEL

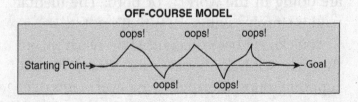

There are many inner signs that help you know when it is time to correct. The two most obvious are confusion and unhappiness. These are seen to be bad rather than good. I know it is hard to accept, but *an upset in your life is a good thing*. It tells you that you are off course in some way, and that you need to find your way back to your correct path once again.

Your confusion and unhappiness are telling you that you're off-track. And, as the Chinese proverb says, 'If you don't change your direction, you're likely to end up where you're heading.'

Physical pain is easily seen as beneficial, even though it can hurt a lot. It is an obvious sign that something is wrong with your body. A pain in your right side might save your life by signalling an appendicitis attack. If you don't pay attention to it, you could die.

Mental pain is just as much a 'blessing', because it is telling you that something is wrong with the way your life is going. It is a sign that something needs to be corrected – whether it is the way you think about the world or what you are doing in the world – or both. The mental pain is simply saying, 'Hey, that's not it!'

You can get back on course by – reaching out through self-help books, workshops, friends, support groups, therapy or whatever seems right for you when you reach out for help. As long as you are open to reaching out, help will be there.

Remember, 'When the student is ready, the teacher will appear.' You will never be ready if you are busy sticking to the course you have chosen for yourself. You will always be off course and never reach your goal. When you are constantly aware of the signs that say 'time to correct', you will always end up in the right spot – or at least close to it.

Now that I've shown the No-Win and No-Lose Models for decision making, I hope you can see how it is impossible to make a mistake. Just as each decision is an opportunity to learn, each 'mistake' is also an opportunity to learn. This is why it is impossible to make a mistake.

A great researcher failed two hundred times before he found the answer to one of his most important questions. He was asked, 'Doesn't it bother you that you failed all those times?' His answer was, 'I never failed! I discovered two hundred ways *not* to do something!'

Exercises

1. Using the No-Lose Model, consider some decisions you are now facing. Write down all the good things that can happen by using either pathway – even if the outcome might not be what you picture.

2. Learn the idea of *it doesn't really matter* by starting with little decisions you face each day. As you think about which shirt to wear to work, notice that it doesn't really matter. Or as you think about what to eat a tonight, notice that it doesn't really matter. Or which film to watch doesn't really matter. Each choice simply produces a different experience. Slowly you will be able to apply this idea to larger and larger decisions. Put signs in your home and place of work that say:

It really doesn't matter

to remind yourself when you are worrying for no reason.

3. Also, put signs in your home and place of work that say:

So what! I'll handle it!

If things don't work out the way you want, so what! What's the big deal, anyway? This reminder will help you relax about life as you learn you can handle whatever happens after you've made your decision.

4. Look at signs in your life that suggest you are off course, and begin making your plan to get back on the path you want.

Chapter 6

Just Nod Your Head – Say 'Yes!'

One of the most valuable lessons in learning to reduce fear is set out in the phrase *'Say yes to your universe'*. These words were casually spoken by Janet Zuckerman, a wonderful teacher, to someone who was complaining bitterly about something that happened to him. I asked Janet exactly what she meant by that phrase.

She replied, 'It's simple. Whatever happens to you in life, just nod your head, up and down, instead of shaking it, side to side. Just say *yes* instead of no.' Over the years I've used these words in my life with magical results.

The word 'universe' refers to that life plan that seems to take over when we were expecting something else. It is the force that seems to work on its own, and that often muddles our picture of how we would like things to be. 'Universe' refers to a certain flow in our lives and the lives of others over which we have little or no control. Often when we are ready to move in a certain direction, an unexpected event changes everything. Those unexpected events, or even knowing that the unexpected is *possible* causes a great deal of fear. We expect the worst. It is important to remember:

The cure for our fear lies in saying 'yes'.

The phrase 'say yes' means 'to agree to' those things that life hands to us. Saying *yes* means not struggling against, but letting in the opportunities that our universe offers of new ways of seeing the world. It means to relax bodily, and calmly survey what has happened. This will reduce upset and worry. As well as being good for the mind, saying 'yes' is good for the body.

On the other hand, saying *no* means to be a victim. 'How could this happen to me!' Saying *no* means to block, to fight, to struggle against opportunities for growth and challenge. Saying *no* creates tension, tiredness, wasted energy, upset feelings, – or, worse, it creates a lack of caring. 'I can't cope. I can't go on. There is no hope.' The truth of the matter is that saying *yes* is our only hope.

Saying *yes* is our cure for day-to-day upsets, rejections, and missed opportunities (the flu, a leaking roof, a traffic jam, a flat tyre, an awful date, and so on). *It is also the miracle tool for dealing with our deepest, darkest fears.*

When I set out the idea of *Say yes to your universe* to my students, one of them asked a clever question: 'If you always say *yes* to your universe, wouldn't you be able to avoid feeling any pain?'

I thought about that for a moment and told him, 'No. You can't avoid pain, but you can say *yes* to the pain, understanding that it is a part of life. You do not, then, feel you are a victim. You know that you can handle the pain, as well as the issue that is causing the pain. You do not feel it is hopeless.'

At that point, my student shouted, 'I get it! You mean there is the pain of *yes* versus the pain of *no*.'

That was exactly what I meant.

As the students looked at it further, they found examples of when they had said *yes* to pain in their lives without realising what they were doing. A student called Nadine remembered one day the previous week when she thought about her mother, who had recently died. Suddenly she was struck by the pain of loss. She sat down and cried, thinking how strangely sweet it felt to remember good times she had shared with her mother. And as she cried, she felt the urge to say 'thanks' over and over again.

She was aware, in the middle of her pain, that life hands you a lot of goodbyes – but that's just the way life is. Yet she saw the difference between handling the death of a loved one as a disaster (saying *no*) and keeping in mind how blessed she was to have had that person in her life (saying *yes*). It is seeing death as part of living – a natural process – instead of seeing it as a horrible loss and an unjust event.

A student called Marge shared with us the pain she felt when her husband died. Yes, she missed her husband and the warmth and friendship he had given her. But she was also aware of how she had changed herself from a dependent to an independent person when left to take care of herself. Her sense of self-esteem had grown hugely as she slowly learned to take risks she had never taken before. She was able to say *yes* to life and create a whole new world for herself.

Marge could have reacted like a friend of mine did. He refused to pick up the pieces and go on after his wife died. Five years later, he is still crying on the phone, asking, 'Why did she have to die?' He has said *no* to his universe. Sadly, he doesn't see that the universe isn't suffering. Only he is suffering, and perhaps the few people who still talk to him on the phone. He has refused to see the blessings in his life – and there are many. He fails to see the opportunities around him to meet new people and try new experiences. The pain of *no* leaves him feeling powerless.

It can be said that your ability to cope well with the world around you matches your ability to say *yes* to your universe, including the pain. Remember:

Accepting pain is very important – rejecting it is deadly.

Sandy is someone who avoided her pain. When her son died in an car accident twelve years ago, she never faced the full impact of the loss. Friends said how well she had handled her son's death. Three years later, she developed epilepsy, which seemed to be unrelated to the loss of her son. For nine years she suffered from fits that stopped her working. At the same time, her relationships with her husband and other children were slowly breaking down.

Sandy finally went to a support group to help her deal with the upset her epilepsy was creating within the family. During the first session, the group leader asked if she had ever suffered a great loss. She said yes, but that it had happened so long ago it was no longer a factor in her life. He knew better and with great skill got her to remember the experience of her son's death. It was then that she finally allowed her grief to surface.

Each time the group met, Sandy continued to deal with her pain. Almost 'like a miracle,' her epilepsy disappeared within five weeks. She stopped her medication, found a good job and began to repair the damage done within her home as a result of her illness. Pain can be very damaging if it is kept hidden. Sandy's pain is a dramatic example, but rejected pain is quietly destroying many people's lives.

We all know people who are out of touch with their pain – who have refused to let themselves feel it. When we don't accept our pain, it will surface as a symptom in our body, or as anger, or as something equally harmful. Saying *yes* means accepting the pain's full force, knowing you will get to the other side of it, *and* gain something in the end – if you look for it.

We are all winners when we say *yes*, and it is worth every effort to learn how. These steps will help:

1. *Be aware* that you are saying *no*. It helps to surround yourself with reminders. Put signs on your desk, on your bedside table, on your mirrors, in your daily calendar, or wherever you'll see them. Some signs that helped me were: Say yes to your universe (an obvious one), or I am finding value in everything that happens to me; let go. My daughter gave me a wonderful poster that read, If life gives you lemons, make lemonade. You can create your own sayings that work best for you. The object is to stay *aware.* We are asleep on this issue and need constantly to be reminded.

2. Once you are aware, *actually nod your head up and down, and say yes.* There is something about asserting an idea physically that helps you to accept it. Try nodding your head right now. You'll notice you feel something good about the feeling of physically nodding. It gives you the sense that everything will be all right – because you are going to make it all right.

3. Using the same idea, physically relax your body, starting from the top of your head

and going to the tip of your toes. Notice where you are tense and focus on letting the tension go. Again the body can take the lead in setting up good feelings.

4. Look for ways to create value from any experience. Ask yourself these questions: what can I learn from the experience? How can I use this experience to gain something? How can I learn to better myself as a result of this experience? Simply having the desire to create something useful will make sure that something useful will happen. As I said in Chapter 5, let go of the picture of what the outcome 'should' be, to open the way for opportunities your mind can't imagine.

5. Be patient with yourself, *Don't say no to your difficulty in saying yes*. This is one of those ideas that seems easy but needs effort to put into practice. It is easy to feel crushed when gloom and doom overtake you. Just keep noticing this. Trust that a time will come when you'll get bored with being depressed or upset. Then you'll find a way out of the gloom. Most of us find a way out anyway. But saying *yes* helps you find your way much faster, and vastly improves the quality of your life.

One more tip may be helpful. Start practising on small events in your life. They may have nothing to do with fear, but they will help you practice the process. For example, as you sit in your car in a rage because of a traffic jam, a sign on the dashboard that reads *Say yes to your universe* may remind you that you are saying *no*. Once you are aware of that, you can nod your head, relax your body and begin to gain something from the experience.

The only time you will fear anything is when you say *no* and resist the universe. You may have heard the words 'Get into the flow'. This means accepting what is happening in your life.

I once heard it said that the key to life is not to work out what you can *get from* the flow, but, rather, to work out how to *get into* the flow. Or, as Barry Stevens titled her book, *Don't Push the River (It Flows by Itself)*. Stop fighting your life. Let go and let the river carry you to new adventures by the way you experience your life. In this way – and only in this way – you cannot lose.

Summary

Steps to saying yes

1. Be aware that you can choose to say *yes* or *no*.
2. Nod your head – say *yes*.
3. Relax your body.
4. Think to yourself 'It's all happening perfectly. Let's see what good I can create from this experience'.
5. Be patient with yourself. It takes times to settle on a 'yes' approach to life. Say *yes* to you!

Chapter 7

Choosing Love and Trust

Do you consider yourself a giving person? Think about it for a moment.

I asked some of my students this question one morning. Most of them were married, and they all nodded their heads, meaning yes. Therefore, they were puzzled by their own reactions to the homework I then gave them. I said simply, 'Go home and say "thank you" to your wives or husbands'.

There was a distinct sense of unease in the room. You would have thought I had asked them to go home and beat their children! Finally, Lottie, who had been married for twenty-five years, said, 'Why should I say thank you to my husband? He should be glad I'm there!'

'Lottie, why *are* you there?' I asked.

Her answer was unclear – something like: 'He'd be a mess without me, and, besides, it would be too much trouble to leave'.

I repeated my question.

After much prompting from me and the other students, Lottie finally was able to accept that her husband gave her a number of good things: friendship, money, security and the feeling that she was not alone.

I said, 'Fine, so go home and thank him for that.'

At the next class the students had looks of dismay on their faces. They couldn't believe how difficult it had been to accept the value of their wives or husbands. Some were able to do the homework, though it had been hard; others simply could not do it at all. Some said that they also tried to thank their children and parents, and that, too, was very difficult. For the first time, they were forced to question just how giving they really were.

This did not mean that they were not valuable in other areas of their relationships. For the most part, they handled the details of the home, raised the children, and performed the essential tasks of the marriage. But were they really giving? Did they really know how to give? Or did they just exchange a 'you do this for me' with an 'I'll do this for you'.

Naturally, my students were quite dismayed by what they had found out about themselves from this simple task. I assured them that most of us do not really know how to give. Most of us work on a hidden exchange system. Few truly ever give anything away without expecting something back – money, thanks, love or whatever.

You might be saying, 'What's wrong with getting back?'

My answer is, 'Nothing.' However:

If all your 'Giving' is about 'Getting',
think how full of fear you will become.

More than likely the question will soon become, 'Am I getting back *enough*?' This kind of thinking sets up a strong need to control others so you won't feel overlooked, or taken for granted. It destroys your peace of mind and creates anger and resentment.

Now you can see what's wrong with 'getting' being the most important reason for 'giving'. In fact:

True giving is not only caring,
it also makes us feel better.

Why do we find it so difficult to give? My answer has two parts. First, only a mature adult can give, and most of us have never really grown up. Second, giving is a learned skill that few of us have picked up.

These two parts are connected and need a great deal of practice to achieve. Most of us have never practised these skills because we haven't realised that we aren't behaving like adults or that we aren't giving. Without knowing it, we have fooled ourselves. And this is not surprising. We *look* like adults and we *seem* to be giving to people. What's really happening, though, is something else.

One of the most important lessons one has to learn in life is how to give, and *in that lesson lies an answer to fear.* As babies we display the basic form of neediness. We come into this world as total takers. We have to take, or we will die. Our survival depends on the world caring for us. We give little back. We don't care what time we wake our parents when we are hungry. Or how loudly we scream and bother the neighbours when we want to be picked up.

Yes, parents often get a feeling of joy from the smile or the touch of their child. In that sense, the child is a giver. But I doubt that the child spent the night thinking: 'My life is full. I have so much to give away. I think I'll reward my parents with a great big smile tomorrow morning.' No, their 'gift' is on a rather simple or non-thinking level. In fact, a hungry belly in the morning will produce only loud shrieks of anger.

As the years pass, we live as more and more independent beings, able to take care of ourselves – or so it appears. We dress ourselves. We feed ourselves. We earn a living. Yet there seems to be a part of us that never moves much beyond the cot. Below the surface, we remain frightened that no one will come to relieve our hunger – for food, money, love, praise and so on. Any relief in the way of 'food' is only brief; we know the hunger will come again.

Imagine how this affects our daily lives. We can't give. We can't love. Either consciously or unconsciously, we become controlling, because the issue is our survival. We can't support the well-being of another person if their needs in any way disagree with ours. And how do we feel working from the level of the playpen? Helpless, trapped, angry, defeated, unhappy, unfulfilled, and, most of all, *fearful*.

What can be more frightening than depending on someone else for one's survival? As fearful adults, we ask the same questions we did as a child. Will they go away and not come back? Will they stop loving me? Will they take care of me? Will they get sick and die? As adults, we ask these questions about our partners, and often about our friends, bosses, parents, and even children.

People who fear can't truly give. They are filled with a deep sense of lack in the world, as if there wasn't enough to go around. Not enough love, not enough money, not enough praise, not enough attention – simply not enough. Usually fear in one area of our lives causes us to become closed down and watchful in many areas of our lives. Fearful people can be imagined as crouched and hugging themselves. This image shows the inner state of all frightened people, but the outer signs can take on many forms:

- Successful businessmen needing the boss's approval.
- Housewives who blame their husbands or children for the fact that they never lived their own lives.
- Independent career women who demand so much from their men that they are often alone.
- Men who can't accept their wives' independence.
- Company executives who make harmful, thoughtless decisions.

They are all in some way working out of a sense of fear for their own survival. They are all, in effect, crouched and holding back inside.

If you recognise yourself in this vision of fearful people, you are just like the rest of us. Few people have actually been taught the secrets of growing up and giving. We have been taught the pretence of giving, but not the actual fact of giving. As we have been taught to take care of our physical safety, we have also been taught not to let anyone trick us or cheat us. As a result, unless we get something back, we feel used.

This is not to say that we can't enjoy what comes back to us, and strangely:

When we give from a place of love, rather than from a place of seeking reward, usually more comes back to us than we could ever have imagined.

But if we are always expecting something back, we will spend a great deal of our lives angry because the world isn't treating us right.

I didn't find my way out of this painful way of life until my mid-thirties. Then, at last, I saw that no matter how much I had in my life, *nothing would ever be enough!* The more

I had, the more I wanted – more love, more money, more praise – more, more, more.

Obviously, something I was or wasn't doing was keeping me from ever feeling satisfied. And, worse, I was in a constant state of fear that everything I had would in the end disappear and there would be nothing left. As the saying goes, I saw everything as the last drink of water in the desert, and I had to own it.

It was time to try another way of being, since my old way was definitely not working for me or anyone else in my life. As I wrote earlier in this book, I found many teachers and got many answers.

Basically, I learned that to get rid of the fear of losing everything, I had to do the *opposite* of what I had been doing up until that time. Instead of hanging on to everything in a bid to survive, I had to start releasing, letting go, giving it away.

If you think anything else in this book is difficult, wait until you try this one! It's easy to give when you feel you have everything, but you only feel that way *when* you give, not before! So: *Feel the fear… and do it anyway!*

Again, let me remind you that this is a lifelong process that you can begin working on today. There is no magical shortcut. It is amazing how long it takes to become a proper adult. In fact, one might consider it a lifelong task. I've been working on it for years and I'm still working on it. The good news, however, is that my sense of personal power and my ability to love and trust have grown at least 1,000 per cent since I have been practising giving it away. Many fears in the areas I write about below have completely disappeared for me. The rewards are huge. I promise!

Give Away Thanks

Start by thinking about the people presently in your life and important ones in your past. Put their names on a sheet of paper. Then list what each of them gave to you in their own special way. Even if they brought you pain, and you very much dislike them, list what they gave to your life. Like Lottie, earlier, who thought, at first, that she had nothing to thank her husband for, there was much that he had provided for her. Also, it's possible to make a gift even out of something bad.

I said sorry to my son one day because, when I got divorced, I wasn't there to support him when he might have needed me. I was too wrapped up in my own pain to help him with his.

His answer was, 'It's okay, Mum. That was the period of my life when I learned independence. That was a valuable lesson.' He was able to thank me for my failure! In terms of mental health, he was far better off than if he had been angry through all those years. So, even if you think that someone has hurt you, find the lesson you learned from them and put that on your list.

This can be very difficult to apply to some people in your life, such as an ex-wife, ex-husband, ex-friends or bosses, or parents or children who have become distant from you. To help rid yourself of nagging feelings of anger, try an exercise I learned in a workshop many years ago:

- Find an empty room and turn off the telephone.
- Put on some soothing music.
- Sit down in a comfortable chair and close your eyes.
- Imagine someone who brings up a lot of anger or pain in you. Picture them in front of you.
- First, surround them with rays of healing white light, and tell them that you wish them all good things – everything they could possibly want in their lifetime.

- Thank them for whatever they have given you.
- Keep doing this until you feel your anger leaving you.

This is not at all easy. In fact it is hugely difficult. 'Wish *her* good things? Are you out of your mind? I want to see her suffer for what she's done to me!'

The first time I did this exercise, I picked someone who had worked for me. He had caused me a great deal of upset and pain. I had trusted him, and, to my mind, he had betrayed me. (Note the victim way of thinking in full flow! Obviously I was not taking charge of my experience of life at that time.) As I went through the exercise, I experienced a strange set of feelings.

First, I was shocked at the anger and resentment I felt. I found it almost impossible, even in my mind's eye, to wish him anything good. At first my anger toward him was huge. As I slowly let the anger go, I found the pain I felt. This turned to anger at myself for allowing what had happened, and for holding all my anger for so long. This turned into forgiveness of myself and of him. I was able to see both of us simply as people who had done the best we could at the time. I could then surround us both with healing white light.

We need to get rid of pain and anger before we can bring in love. When we hold bad feelings about people in our past, we carry those feelings to people in our present. Not only that, but we can make ourselves physically ill, as some of you may have already experienced.

An excellent book to read on the subject of healing your body and mind is Louise Hay's *You Can Heal Your Life*. She has many exercises that will help you release the anger, pain and resentment that you may be carrying around with you.

Give Away Information

So much of what we learn in life comes to us after a great struggle. And, for some reason, we tend to want to see others struggle as much as we did. I suggest you turn this around and begin giving others as much help as you possibly can. In your work, this can be very difficult. I can remember times when I felt that I was competing with those I felt were my rivals. I wanted to keep back information that would help them in their work.

Thank goodness, I felt the fear ... and did it anyway. I shared information. Some of the people I helped have become my good friends and part of my support system. Here, too, the giving has to be done with no wish to get something back. It is likely, though, that the return will be enormous.

One of my students asked what would have happened if one of them really had turned against me, and had used my information to compete with my work.

My answer was, and is, what do I have to fear if I have enough belief in myself to know that I will do well whatever anyone does? It's a matter of developing trust in yourself and in your universe. For some reason, when you become a support to others you become bigger than you are. Also, when people use what they have learned from you, your impact on this world becomes greater.

Give Away Praise

For many of us, the people we find hardest to praise are those closest to us – our partners, our children, our parents and sometimes our friends. A lot of the difficulty comes from anger and resentment. Yet, in some strange way, when we praise the people in our lives, we lose the anger and open the door for their being loving toward us.

Many people who are in relationships focus on those aspects of their partners that they dislike. And then they find it easy to tell their partners what they are doing wrong. It is no wonder so few relationships are going well. We want our loved ones to be supportive and comforting. It is important to surround ourselves with giving, loving and caring people. This suggests the other side of the coin:

You must become what you want to attract. Be the kind of person you want to surround yourself with.

Give Away Love

I believe that all of the 'give aways' I have mentioned are about giving away love. But there are other strands to loving. For example, when we let someone be who they are without trying to change them, that is giving away love. When we trust that someone can handle his or her own life, and leave them to get on with it, that is giving away love. When we let go and allow others to learn and grow without feeling that they are competing with us, that is giving away love. How many relationships do you know that look like that?

What often looks like love is not – it is need. Rollo May wrote in *Man's Search For Himself*, 'Love is generally confused with dependence, but in point of fact, you can love only in proportion to your capacity for independence.'

**To love is to be able to give.
And now is the time to begin.**

I've suggested giving away thanks, information, praise, time and, now, love. I'm sure you can think of other things to add to the list. You now understand that giving is about flowing outwards. It is about letting go of your crouched self that holds back, and instead standing tall with your arms stretched out. When we really feel this sense of abundance, of having plenty to give, we truly understand the saying 'My cup runs over.'

Giving from the belief that you count adds to your ability to give. Like any other skill, however, it takes practice.

Whether you believe it or not, your life is already abundant – by which I mean filled with good things. You simply haven't noticed it. Before you can accept abundance in your life, you have to notice it.

One way to increase your awareness is through what I call The Book of Abundance. Buy yourself a notebook. Start filling it by listing as many good things in your life – past and present – as you can think of. Don't stop until you reach 150. Some people will find more. When you feel you can't think of any more, realise that you can find more. Just keep focusing on all the blessings in your life. No matter how small they seem, put them in your book.

Each day make entries in your book. For many people a normal diary is made up of doom and gloom, wish and want. Instead of that kind of diary, create this book, which in effect simply states, 'I have!' Note every positive thing, large or small, that happens – a compliment from a friend, a cheerful hello from the postman, a beautiful sky, a chance to help someone, a haircut, a new suit, nourishing food. *Notice* everything wonderful that happens to you.

If you do this, I suspect you will have a cupboard full of such books in a very short time. Look at them often – especially when you are feeling that you lack something. Lack is only in the mind. Some of the greatest givers I ever met were the poor I met at The

Floating Hospital. I watched them and their sense of what they gave to the people in their community, and it was joyous. Lack is not about money or things, it is about love. And love is always there for you to create when you are conscious that...

Your life is abundant, and you count!

Keep remembering that you are aiming to get to the point where you are the giver. When you are aware that 'you have', you can give. When you are a giver, you have nothing to fear. You are powerful and you are loving. The trick in life is not working out what you can get, but what you can give. There is so much power in this kind of thinking that it surprises the imagination.

Think about this – if you see that your purpose in life is to give, then it's almost impossible for anyone to trick you into parting with something. If someone takes, they are simply fulfilling your life's purpose, and they deserve your thanks. When you act the giving adult, your fears are reduced ... you realise you are meant to be used.

Chapter 8

There Is Plenty of Time

There you sit ... filled with all sorts of advice about how to make yourself powerful in the face of all your fears. What's next? What can I say to you to help keep you on course as you continue on the next part of your journey? First, the strength and encouragement you have already gained from this book will always be here for you whenever you need it. When you feel you are going off course, or are being battered by outside forces, come back and read again the parts that make you feel good.

The biggest hazard as you make your way through life is impatience. Remember that being impatient is simply a way of punishing yourself. It creates stress, unhappiness and fear. Whenever your Chatterbox is making you feel impatient, ask it, 'What's the rush? It's all happening perfectly. Don't worry. When I am ready to move forward, I will. In the meantime, I am taking it all in and I am learning.'

When we wake up to the possible power inside us, our impulse is to grab it all quick. But the more we grab, the more it seems to escape from us. There is no quick. There are quick – and wonderful – lectures, workshops, books, and CDs that give you tools, but they are not quick tools. They are to be used and studied through a lifetime.

Our impatience reminds me of a time when my son was a little boy. I showed him how to plant a seed in a flowerpot and said that soon, from the little seed, a beautiful flower would appear. I left him with his flowerpot and went off to do other things.

Much later I went back to his room and saw he had placed a chair in front of the flowerpot and was sitting there watching it. I asked him what he was doing, and he said, 'I'm waiting for the flower to appear.' I realised I had missed something out when I told him about the seed and the flower. So don't let me do the same thing to you.

Often when we are feeling low, thinking that we are learning nothing from all our efforts, changes are really taking place within us. We become aware of them long after they have been going on. In the end, my son did have his flower. One day he awoke and it was there. Although it didn't look as if anything was happening, it was. And so it is with you.

One day, I threw a log on the glowing embers of a dying fire and went back to the book I was reading. From time to time, I'd glance over at the fire and notice that there was no flame yet. There wasn't even the smoke that often signals a fire to come. Then, as I stared at a fire that seemed dead, flames suddenly burst out around the log. Patience means knowing it will happen … and giving it time to happen.

Again, it requires *Trust* – trust that it is all happening perfectly. What do I mean by 'perfectly'? I have come to believe there are only two kinds of experiences in life, those that come from our Higher Self and those that have something to teach us. We know the first as pure joy and the second as struggle. But they are both perfect.

Each time we come up against some intense difficulty, we know there is something we haven't learned yet, and the universe is now giving us the opportunity to learn. If we go through the experience with this in mind, all the 'victim' is taken out of the issue, and we allow ourselves to say *yes*. So, no matter what is happening at any time in your life, keep in mind that it is all perfect.

As long as you can remember that life is a continuing process of learning, you won't have the annoying feeling that you haven't made it yet. My experience of the last few years has shown me that so much of the joy in life is the task of working it all out. Nothing is as pleasing as those moments when you find out something about yourself and the universe that solves another part of the puzzle. The joy of finding out is magical. I know of no person who once having reached his or her goal has not wanted to go out and find something more.

The task is to stay on the Path of the Higher Self. It is a far more enjoyable path than the others you may choose to follow. You will know if you are on the right path by the way you feel. Trust your feelings. If the path you're on isn't giving you joy, peace, vision, love and caring, it's not the right path. Say to yourself, 'Okay, I tried this, and this isn't it. What else can I try?' Don't be tricked into thinking that by changing what is outside, what is inside will be changed. It works the other way around.

The path that needs changing is the one in your mind. Once you become lined up with your Higher Self, you may still want to change things in your physical world. But it is your mind that has to be changed first – then all that is right will follow.

The Path is much like climbing a mountain. The climb is tough. But each time you stop to look around, the view becomes better. You see a greater sweep, and the flaws of the world below disappear as you see more and more of the view. As you climb higher, you leave the heavy load below. You feel lighter. You feel freer. And you are lifted higher by the growing beauty around you.

From this place, you become more caring as well. You may greatly dislike some people for their cruel behaviour. But from a higher place, you'll see more of the whole. These people are more than their poor behaviour. They, too, have a fine place inside, which they haven't found yet. So you'll begin to feel their sadness and not be so harsh in your judgment.

The journey upward is not always a steady climb. You may climb, then stop and rest, and make plans. So, too, with your spiritual climb. Sometimes it may seem as though you have stopped growing. This is not so. You are just sorting out your information.

Some of what you learn may mean that you drop beliefs and behaviour that have been part of you since you were born. Sometimes you'll experience an *aha!* moment, and change will seem instant. Again, this is not so. Sudden understanding is the result of all that has happened before. Your Subconscious Mind, like a computer, searches and sorts without you knowing it and, when you least expect it, comes up with the answer.

Sudden understanding happens more often, however, the farther along the journey you are. The Conscious Mind lets go of its struggle against new ways of thinking. It develops more trust. The early stages are the most difficult and need the greatest focus.

Sometimes when you think you've finally 'got it', the universe will step in to show you haven't. I've adopted a phrase of Lena Horne's that keeps me humble: 'I've come a long way ... maybe!' I have learned that there is always more to learn. And experience is our greatest teacher. There is so much excitement and wonder in front of you. Sometimes you will experience the joy of being in the flow. Sometimes you will experience the pain of being way off course. Remember you are not alone. This world is filled with support systems that are there for the taking, whenever you are feeling troubled by life's experiences.

One of my students said to me, 'I read and read, and I assume one day one of those books is going to take!'

I replied immediately, 'No. *Nothing is going to take unless you take it!!*' And so it is with this book and with every source. *Don't wait for it to take! Take it!* Use it. Live it. Take it in. Unless you use the muscle that lifts you to your Higher Self, it will weaken – just as your body weakens when it is not used. If you think you need more help, then by all means, go to a teacher. Take action. Nothing is going to work for you unless you do the work.

Say *yes* to life. Join in. Move. Act. Write. Read. Sign up. Take a stand. Or do whatever works for you. Get involved in the process. Rollo May wrote in *Man's Search for Himself*: 'Every organism has one and only one central need in life, to fulfil its own potentialities.' He went on to say that joy is the result of using our powers to the full, and for that reason, joy, not happiness, is the goal of life.

And what is joy? It is something that expresses the cheerful side of the spiritual part of ourselves. Joy is made from lightness, humour, laughter and fun. Lighten up. If you have ever been around a person who is centred and enlightened, you are struck by their humour and ability to laugh at themselves. All the edges are gone and only an easy flow remains.

So commit! Commit yourself to pushing through the fear and becoming more than you are at the present moment. The you that could be is absolutely vast. You don't need to change what you are doing – simply commit to learning how to bring to whatever you do in life the loving and powerful energy of your Higher Self. Whether you are a bank cashier, housewife, business executive, student, street cleaner, teacher, film producer, salesman, lawyer, or whatever, it's yours to give.

As you live this way, moment by moment, day by day, in perfect time, you will find yourself moving closer and closer to Home. The mystery is that when you stay close to Home, you can go anywhere and do anything without fear. The Divine Homesickness disappears as you find the place where we all are connected as loving human beings. Whatever it takes to get you there, *Feel the fear and do it anyway!*

About Quick Reads

Quick Reads are brilliant short new books written by bestselling writers. They are perfect for regular readers wanting a fast and satisfying read, but they are also ideal for adults who are discovering reading for pleasure for the first time.

Since Quick Reads was founded in 2006, over 4.5 million copies of more than a hundred titles have been sold or distributed. Quick Reads are available in paperback, in ebook and from your local library.

To find out more about Quick Reads titles, visit
www.readingagency.org.uk/quickreads
Tweet us 🐦 @Quick_Reads

Quick Reads is part of The Reading Agency,
a national charity that inspires more people to read more, encourages them to share their enjoyment of reading with others and celebrates the difference that reading makes to all our lives.
www.readingagency.org.uk Tweet us @readingagency

The Reading Agency Ltd • Registered number: 3904882 (England & Wales) Registered charity number: 1085443 (England & Wales) Registered Office: Free Word Centre, 60 Farringdon Road, London, EC1R 3GA The Reading Agency is supported using public funding by Arts Council England.

We would like to thank all our funders:

LOTTERY FUNDED

Quick Reads has something for everyone

Stories to make you laugh

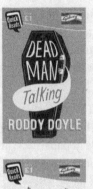

Stories to make you feel good

Stories to take you to another place

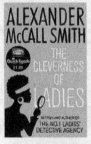

Stories about real life

Stories to take you to another time

Stories to make you turn the pages

For a complete list of titles visit

www.readingagency.org.uk/quickreads

Available in paperback, ebook and from your local library

Discover the pleasure of reading with Galaxy®

Curled up on the sofa,
Sunday morning in pyjamas,
just before bed,
in the bath or
on the way to work?

Wherever, whenever,
you can escape
with a good book!

So go on...
indulge yourself with
a good read and the
smooth taste of
Galaxy® chocolate.

Proudly
supports

Start a new chapter

One False Move

Dreda Say Mitchell

Hayley swore when she got out of prison that
she would turn her life around.

But living on the Devil's Estate doesn't make that easy.

She spends her days looking after her daughter, and her nights
collecting cash from people who can't get loans any other way.

But someone has just robbed her. And she has twenty-four
hours to get the money back, or her boss will come for her.

Her criminal ex-boyfriend says he can help.
Hayley wants nothing to do with him. But time is running out,
and she has to choose – save herself, or save her soul?

If she makes one false move, her life will be over . . .

Available in paperback, ebook and from your local library

Start a new chapter

Looking for Captain Poldark

Rowan Coleman

Four strangers, united by their shared love of
POLDARK, come together on a trip to Cornwall
in search of their hero ...

Lisa has sworn off love and relationships after a really
bad experience, but lately she's been tempted to take a chance
on a more exciting life. First she meets other fans of the
TV show *Poldark* online. Then she proposes a very
special road trip to Cornwall, in search of where
their favourite show is being filmed.

But can four strangers find friendship,
as well as a certain sexy hunk on their trip south?

Available in paperback, ebook and from your local library

Start a new chapter

The Other Side of You

Amanda Craig

Will must run, or die. He's seen a murder,
and the gang on his estate are after him.

Hurt, hungry and afraid, he comes to an abandoned house in
a different part of the city. Behind its high fences is a place of
safety. Here, he can hide like a wounded beast. He can find
food, and healing – and learn how to do more than survive.

But when Will meets Padma, he must choose between his good
side and his bad one. For the gang he left behind is still there.
How can he live without becoming a killer?
How can he love without being a thief?

Exciting, fast-paced and different, this is a story
that keeps you reading until the last line.

Available in paperback, ebook and from your local library

Start a new chapter

A Very Distant Shore

Jenny Colgan

**Wanted: doctor for small island. Must like boats,
the seaside and having no hope of keeping a secret...**

Lorna lives on the tiny Scottish island of Mure,
a peaceful place where everyone helps their neighbour.
But the local GP is retiring, and nobody wants his job.
Mure is too small and too remote.

Far away, in a crowded camp, Saif is treating a little boy
with a badly-cut hand. Saif is a refugee, but he's
also a doctor: exactly what Mure needs.

Saif is welcome in Mure, but can he forget his past?
Over one summer, Saif will find a place to call home,
and Lorna's life will change forever.

Available in paperback, ebook and from your local library

Start a new chapter

Feel the Fear and Do It Anyway®

Susan Jeffers

Is there something holding you back from becoming the person you want to be?

Fear is all around us, from having a tricky talk with your boss to facing up to a problem at home.

Everyone has worries and fears that can stop them progressing and reaching for the things that they really want in life.

The simple, life-changing exercises in *Feel the Fear and Do It Anyway*® will teach you how to turn anger into love and uncertainty into action.

Available in paperback, ebook and from your local library

Start a new chapter

Dead Simple

Eight killer reads from eight bestselling authors

Edited by Harry Bingham

Dead Simple is a thrilling collection of short stories from some of the best crime writers around. The stories include the perfect murder and an unusual way to solve crimes. From prison cells to cosy living rooms, these dark, chilling tales will grip you with every twist and turn.

This collection includes specially written short crime fiction from Mark Billingham, Clare Mackintosh, James Oswald, Jane Casey, Angela Marsons, Harry Bingham, Antonia Hodgson and CL Taylor.

Available in paperback, ebook and from your local library